# Falling Back

3/9/18

Dan (and Cindy?)
Hope some of these
poems speak to you.

Blessings!
Carol

# Falling Back

*Poems by Carol L. Gloor*

Word Poetry

© 2018 by Carol L. Gloor

Published by Word Poetry
P.O. Box 541106
Cincinnati, OH 45254-1106

ISBN: 9781625492739

Poetry Editor: Kevin Walzer
Business Editor: Lori Jareo

Visit us on the web at www.wordpoetrybooks.com

# Publication Credits

The following poems were first published in the indicated journals, some in hard copy, some online and some as slightly different versions:

1959 in *Baseball Bard*

Antebellum; Pallbearer; Small Things in *Electric Wire Pen*

Anniversary 40 in *St. Sebastian Review*

Annunciation in Northern Illinois in *Vineyards*

Antidepressants in *The Perch*

Baskets in *Stymie Magazine*

Beets; The Starting of the Self in *Highland Park Poetry*

By the Fire; To my Heart; The Woods of Home in *Sage Woman*

Chaco Canyon in *Tallgrass Press*

City by Water in *Rust Belt Chicago*

Corn in *Common Ground*

Dandelions in *Rivverrun*

Dia de Los Muertos in *East on Central*

Ducks in *The Urban Coaster*

Dominion of Light in *Trajectory*

Heaven in *Shark Reef*

How to Survive Winter in *Cram 9*

Florida Keys in *Sow's Ear*

Jackie Deering is Dead in *Gemini*, under a different title

January Afternoon in *Front Porch Review*

Jonquils; Snow; Voyager Enters Deep Space in *Helen Presents*

Leper in *The Illinois State Poetry Society*, under a different title

Lime Jello in *Pure Francis*

Luke 25: 36-42 in *Christian Century*

Scrubbing in *Earth's Daughters*, under a different title

Siberian Sunbathers in *Two Cities Review*

Sparrows in *The Kerf*

Three Screws in *Slant*

To Solitude in *DuPage Valley Review*

To the Carmelite Nuns of Terre Haute, Indiana in *Tipton Poetry Journal*

To John, forever

## Table of Contents

I. CARBON

Snow..............................................................................................15
Wedding Picture............................................................................16
1959...............................................................................................18
My Viet Nam..................................................................................20
Pallbearer.......................................................................................22
School Christmas Concert: December, 1989...................................23
Lime Jello.......................................................................................24
The Starting of the Self..................................................................25
On the Tenth Anniversary of My Mother's Death..........................26
Heaven...........................................................................................27
Night in Room 1006......................................................................28
To My Heart..................................................................................29
After Surgery.................................................................................30
Visit...............................................................................................31
Ash................................................................................................33
To Solitude....................................................................................34
Falling Back...................................................................................35
You Cannot Call Yourself a Nature Lover.....................................36
Dandelions....................................................................................38
Dominion of Light........................................................................39
St. Lucy's Night.............................................................................40
Beaver............................................................................................41
To the Carmelite Nuns of Terre Haute, Indiana............................42
Incarnation....................................................................................43
Manicure.......................................................................................44
Beets..............................................................................................45
Clearing Brush..............................................................................47
Above Miami.................................................................................48

II. CHICAGO

Leper .............................................................................................51
Sleeping on the El.........................................................................52
Antidepressants.............................................................................54

At Hancock Fabrics..................................................................55
Karaoke at the Glenway Tap..................................................57
Caroling at Clark St. Rehabilitation Center.........................58
Scrubbing..................................................................................60
November.................................................................................61
Advent: The Cook County Treasurer's Office.....................62
Bread.........................................................................................63
January Afternoon...................................................................65
On the Sill................................................................................66
Missing Snow...........................................................................67
How to Survive Winter...........................................................69
Ducks........................................................................................70
Winter Rain..............................................................................72
City by Water...........................................................................73
Monet in Chicago....................................................................75
Watching the Cubs in 2003....................................................76
Sparrows...................................................................................78
Napping by the Radiator........................................................79
The Old Woman Rides the Subway......................................80
December..................................................................................81
Darkness...................................................................................83
Anniversary 40.........................................................................84
On the Red Line......................................................................85

## III. CROSSING

Baskets......................................................................................89
Jackie Deering is Dead............................................................91
By the Fire................................................................................92
Pine Lake..................................................................................93
The Woods of Home..............................................................94
A Brief Season.........................................................................96
Right of Way............................................................................98
Chaco Canyon........................................................................100
Siberian Sunbathers...............................................................101
Florida Keys............................................................................103
Antebellum..............................................................................104
The Civil War Memorial in Byron, Illinois.........................106
Just Summer...........................................................................107
An Old Woman at Cancun...................................................109

The House of Old Age ................................................................. 110
Small Things ............................................................................. 111
Dia de Los Muertos .................................................................. 112
March Sunset ............................................................................ 114
Common ................................................................................... 115
Thursday Night ......................................................................... 117
Annunciation in Northern Illinois ............................................ 118
Corn .......................................................................................... 119
three screws .............................................................................. 120
Broken ...................................................................................... 121
Luke 24: 36-42 ......................................................................... 122
Deer in Town ............................................................................ 124
Jonquils ..................................................................................... 125
Voyager Enters Deep Space ..................................................... 126

# I.

# CARBON

# Snow

Two more inches fall the fourth day
after my father's funeral, the day
I can't find my scarf, the red one
my mother crocheted,
and I panic.
But I have done this business before, of living
no matter what, in every season.
In winter, wear boots everyday
and do not forget the house keys.
The cold does not forgive.
Every other day, two inches more snow,
a record forty by the end of February.
One night the first week of March a gale
rattles the windows, the radio says six inches
by morning. In sleep
I see my parents
in a booth at Carson's Restaurant, after church,
(before I knew the boy who loves me still).
They order burger specials for a buck twenty-five.
I bend to embrace them, smelling his Old Spice,
her Wind Song, bending
as we all disappear.

# Wedding Picture

The grandmother I never saw,
folded in Victorian lace, leans
next to the grandfather I saw once.
She is a head taller than him.
Her elegant hands touch
no part of him.

I hung the picture above
the piano for years, my father
sometimes sharing stories:
*She went to convent college, then married*
*an auto worker so she wouldn't be an old maid.*
*She read me* <u>Ivanhoe</u> *and St. Augustine.*

*I understood nothing--maybe you will.*
Later my father told me the troubles:
the screaming and hitting, the cops
feeding him ice cream while
he hid under the table.
How grandpa put her in the asylum,
how she ran away, a Catholic woman
leaving her children in 1931 with only a letter.

She comes to me in darkness, whispering
*I had my books, my music, the pictures*
*of my children I would never see again,*
*their faces almost alive in sunlit afternoons.*

# 1959

I spent the summer alone
with grandpa's cigarette glow
and the TV, where the White Sox
clawed past the Yankees
for the pennant, where the still life
of baseball exploded into the dance
of double play, or stealing second.
I remember their names:
Fox, Aparicio, Landis.
Twice we went to Comiskey.
Off at 35th street, grandpa's arm
around me because it was what
he called a Negro neighborhood.
Then they went west and lost it all.

It would be decades before
they won again. I ditched work
for the ticker tape parade
where sad Chicago finally
cheered, got drunk.
But a few years later,
I can't remember their names.

But the green diamonds,
the freezing opening days,
the October disappointments
are old friends with me,
every season, every year.

# My Viet Nam

At a party where everyone got high,
Michael, the smartest boy
who could not get into college,
said he was going to Nam.
Next morning I saw him alone
on the train platform.
He died there like many later at home,
believing motorcycles could outrun memories.

In April, returning from a class in Renaissance Literature,
I prayed, as always, through the dreaded mail,
searching for one Return Address, Selective Service,
drafting my boy husband, learning anatomy
by dissecting fetal pigs, to become a teacher.
My frozen fingers did not know
I carried a child.

Six years later, on a high blue
day of crocuses, new grass, tight buds,
after walking my son to first grade,
I heard TV news of the final ones
lifted from roofs by helicopters,

their drone stronger than bombs, artillery, screaming,
as they lifted the last of thousands.
My son, home from school,
asked *what's this about?*

Although I grieved the many dead
I answered *I don't know.*

# Pallbearer

I knew my son was grown up
at the funeral of my father,
when he read Yeats:
*tread softly, because you tread on my dreams,*
my father's dreams, a man with polio
asking my mother to dance in 1942
at the Aragon Ballroom, asking her
if she wanted another when
she finished her root beer.

I knew when he grasped one of the brass handles
on the coffin, with the other family men,
and bore it into sunlight,
carried it, with the others, to final ground.
I knew when his hand cupped my elbow,
helping me up the muddy slope.

# School Christmas Concert: December, 1989

Fifteen years ago I left my children in this battered brick mountain, this graffitied, paint-peeling, shouting school, to learn to read and write. I left my daughter in trembling pigtails, my son with brave pencils, and went to work. They teased his red hair, but he learned multiplication and friendship. They ignored her dyslexia and called her lazy, but she learned history and how Ramona cried when her mother was busted for drugs. Now my daughter says, *They never had a Christmas Concert when I was here; they didn't even have music*, but we go anyway. On the coldest night of the year, the auditorium is packed with parents in steaming secondhand wool and down ski jackets, layers of gentrification. The air flashes with cameras, erupts in applause as the voices of children deck these broken halls. Of course we parents understand the die is cast by the time they're six months and it is all over by a year, but when Philip Ramirez, whose voice has not changed, sings *Ave Maria* to our sudden silence, we know why we have come all faithful on this night of crunching snow, burning stars and rumors of live birth. We believe, against all odds, that these unfinished voices will ransom captive Israel, these voices of children floating like birds above the laughing jackals of time.

# Lime Jello

Years ago I read Camus:
he wrote you could live trapped
in a tree trunk, immobile,
so long as there was a hole for seeing,
eyes for looking up
to see the sky change,
the clouds move across.
I thought I understood.

Last month my friend had a stroke
in the dressing room at Macy's.
Two hours before they found her.
She cannot move, speak, write.
The lime jello drops from her mouth.
Her son says she came to him in a dream
and said *kill me*, still
I am always her friend:
her eyes look up,
watch for changes.

# The Starting of the Self

My seven year old granddaughter has a purse,
a little cloth bag, light purple, stuffed
with stickers of *Dora the Explorer* and *Hello Kitty*,
five one dollar bills, folded
and weak from handling,
a quarter, two dimes, four pennies.
In the American Girl Store she wants
the hundred and twenty-five dollar doll,
and gives me all her money to buy her.
I try to explain why not.

If you are reading this
one hundred years from now
you will not know *Dora* or *Hello Kitty* or *American Girl;*
you might not know *dollar*.
No matter. It is the old story of beginnings:
gathering, counting, longing.

# On the Tenth Anniversary of My Mother's Death

I save the heart shaped pillow onto which someone
had stitched yellow letters of her name: *L-E-O-N-A*.
Red poplin front, flower print back, bordered in cheap eyelet lace.

For the first four years I left it on the couch,
but finally moved it to my bed.
It's good support for reading
and fits neatly under my low back
on nights of pain, but mostly
in the dark, sleepless hours
I hold it to my face, surrounding myself
with all that is left of her fragrance:
vague lavender, kitchens, fear.

# Heaven

For me: a train forever west, fragrance of old steel, engine smoke.
By day, the view car: wraparound glass and free chardonnay,
    always west through fields of new corn,
    muscled mountains, whitewater river,
    occasional deer, cinnamon feathered ducklings.
By night, the compartment, my reflection in the black window.
    I always sleep well: rocking,
    constellation stars, occasional moon, sometimes
    the purple curtain of *aurora borealis*.

And on the way Heaven always stops at Hastings, Nebraska.
At four a.m. I hear their kind Midwestern English,
helping each other with baggage, and always
a glimpse of my mother, twenty years old like the photo,
before the emphysema, the terror, the feeding tubes,
my mother in a flowerprint dress and lightly permed hair,
smoking a Chesterfield, flirting with the porters,
eager to come aboard.

# Night in Room 1006

I refuse the urethra catheter,
fearing murderous germs climbing
the plastic tube to my bladder,
so every three hours I have to press
the red button and ask *bedpan*.
I arrange my embarrassed
paper gown so the man
who arrives in the dark,
who never turns on the light,
the man who slips the pan under,
as he and I lift my butt,
will not have to see it.
We both hear the flow,
know when it is finished
so he can leave.
I never see his face:
still I want to thank him
for no questions,
for his silent skills.

# To My Heart

On the metal table
in the white room
with one window
to a closed sky
I see you for the first time
a pulsating fist
on a grainy screen
*whoosh thud thud*

I know they will stop you
saw open my sternum
reach inside you
to replace the small valve
I hate their hands
I want to hold you
red bloody close enough
to hear your answers

*How many beats so far?*
*How many more?*

# After Surgery

You say *come to bed love, even now,*

only four nights after I'm home
from the hospital, my knee
bandaged, pulsing with pain.

You say *come to bed*, and I do,
even though I cannot wrap my legs
around yours, still I know
your hands, lips, the slow rising,

the letting go. You say *come to bed*
after only four nights,
to help me remember I still have the key
to that inlaid wooden box

wherein lies the burnished ruby
nestled in brown velvet. You say
*come to bed* to help me remember
I have not lost the key.

# Visit

I am only her friend.
Her children don't bother
because she won't cooperate,
won't stop drinking, sneaking
cigarettes. She's six feet
tall, ninety-five pounds,
penetrated with tubes
masking any speech.
So I tell her:  *it's cold outside*;
*I'm crocheting a scarf;*
*the governor has been arrested*,
and remind her how she sang
 *Feliz Navidad* at the Christmas concert,
hum her favorite hymn,
push aside her filthy hair,
smooth her papery forehead,

when I leave, whisper
*wish I could do more.*

She dies alone, five hours later.
In four days her body is burned.

# Ash

What happens between the untethering of the tubes
and the cardboard box of lumpy ash?

Whose hands wash the body?
Who drives it to the platform?

Is it only one body, or five. stacked
like cordwood, waiting to be burned?

Who lights the fire?
Does it burn on a metal bench or a stone slab?

What color is the smoke?
Whose hands scrape the ash into the box?

Is the right way to honor remains to
open the box, taste ash on your tongue?

To draw a white line on your forehead
of earthly flesh, sprung from stars?

## To Solitude

Alone all day, I long for her.
Twilight softens the alley outside my window.
I shut down the computer, silence the phones.
As she enters in soft slippers
I notice one bird singing
an octave higher than another.
I watch the window for the moon:
crescent, quarter or full.
She takes my hand, washes my hair,
files my nails, leads me to my chair.
She hands me a walking stick to climb over
the mountain of thoughts into the valley
of sleep, from which I awaken at home
in the world, under whatever moon.

# Falling Back

Everything carbonizes:

    brown leaves drifting,
        then snow crushed,
            finally humus;

    wounded deer
        red walking, staggering,
            then bone fragments, dust;

    our bodies, fueled and used:
        eating, walking, climbing
            the mountain of days,

finally tired, dreaming
of fire.

# You Cannot Call Yourself a Nature Lover

Unless:

    you can embrace these gull chicks
    forced to first flight from arctic nests
    across stony broken ground
    to the life-giving sea;

    you can cherish that some
    will carry their feathered hearts
    to the summer waves,
    and others will feel
    their necks break,
    their breasts burst
    by the ravening teeth
    of an already sated fox;

    you can welcome,
    when three a.m. glows
    on your bedside clock,
    that very fox as he
    scratches your door;

      you can see a last scrap
      of bloody feather
      in his smile and still

open your robe saying
*how nice to see you,*
*my only, my paramour,*
*my all.*

## Dandelions

You call us *weeds*, meaning plants you don't like,
forgetting the Old French ancestry of our name,
*dents de lion*, teeth of the lion,
meaning our jagged leaves

that some still use in salads,
forgetting our other gentle ways:
children gathering our bright flowers
in jars of water, proudly displayed to parents

who sometimes notice our light wine fragrance;
how our bright yellow heads have hidden
under many chins, revealing
who likes butter, and who does not;

forgetting how we turn to light puffs,
the pleasure of blowing us away.
Only to return next season,
next and next and next,

Spring's confetti,
profuse celebration.

# Dominion of Light

The October leaves of locust trees
dangle loosely, a million
golden paper clips. In four days
they will be sidewalk drifts,
blown off, trampled into houses.
So lie beneath them this day.
Enter the dominion of light.

The days of fat chlorophyll are over;
the time of unfurling buds distant
across the mountains of winter.
So lie beneath the locust trees this day.
They hold low-slanted, post equinox
light in the midst of their deaths.
They bequeath only
what they give this day.

## St. Lucy's Night

The opossum freezes near the porch,
caught in my sudden brights,
her eyes huge with terror.
I have heard them called
God's mistake: sack-bodied,
weak-limbed, short-lived.

I douse the lights and step
outside into the cold,
wanting only to whisper apologies,
to stroke her like a cat, to forget
for an instant she is wild.

But she scurry-waddles away,
her naked tail trailing in the porchlight.
I hope she is headed to a warm nest
that smells like her, some safety,
some home, to shelter her through this,
the year's longest night.

# Beaver

The flooding Mississippi
buoys him to the trees
in Riverside Park, waters rising
enough for him to swim
to the young maple
which others of his kind
have already marked
with white gashes.

Huge eyes, patient teeth
gnawing past midnight,
then sliding away,
fat tale powering
his furred body
into muddy darkness,
leaving the old legacy
of how the world goes on.

# To the Carmelite Nuns of Terre Haute, Indiana

I am enclosing twenty-five dollars, all I believe
I can afford, being past sixty and saving
for something, I forget what.

I'll try to send more later, especially for the renovation
of your kitchen and the care of your old ones.
In the meantime, if you remember, pray for me.

I do still try to keep my house clean, but for what
I'm not sure. I polish my bedside table and put
your little card there, the one about the Lord
showing the simple His way,

and sometimes in the night it helps,
and also to imagine you in Terre Haute,
your convent on the high earth above the Wabash.
Especially about five when I panic

at the coming day, it helps to think of you there,
free of the disappointments of children,
imagining you are washed, kneeling,
beginning Matins.

# Incarnation

He came through the vaginal canal
like us all, into her arms, sharp
smell of hay, breath of cows.
Much later, after it had all started,
the dark animal of sleep smothered him
in the boat, so deep the others had to wake him;
and later, thirst, so bad he had to ask
the Samaritan woman for help;
and then hunger, eating
with whores and sharpies;
then, toward Jerusalem, the touch
of Magdalene's hair, ointment on his feet.
When he knew, finally, how it would end,
came the anxious sweat, so rank
the others choked as he rebuked them
for their sleep in the garden.
*Like you never have*, thought Peter.
The nails broke the small bones
of his hands, and hanging, he saw her,
the woman out of whose body he came,
so many years ago, the beginning
of the long story of the flesh.

# Manicure

No occasion looms, only my need
for some part of my old body
to be perfumed, strange,
even beautiful.

So I bring her my hands, my fingers,
my blunt cut nails, some wounded
with shredded cuticles, my nails
with the square faces of simple workers.

I bring her my hands and for twenty dollars
she first gentles them into warm water,
massages, then smoothes them
with gardenia lotion.

Then she tidies with small
silver tools, carefully polishes
in clear rose acrylic, the honest labor
of healing human hands.

# Beets

How did the first gatherers even
know this was food?

Carrots at least tinge orangy red,
maybe reminiscent of early apples;

potatoes wear thin skin
jackets and hum *open, eat me.*

Who knows how a beet looked then?
But pull one up now:

a dirty mass with a snake tail
root hanging from its bottom.

If you didn't know, you wouldn't bother
to take it to your kitchen,

chop off leaves and root, peel;
but with the first cut you learn

your garden has been growing

clandestine rubies, secret garnets:

purple spirals to the center of the universe.

# Clearing Brush

God is resting in a crook of yellow
willow branches against the bluest sky,
an arpeggio of sparrows.

As always: no instructions, no promises.
Just the wind's voice: *today I am
yellow blue everlasting*.

On the last day I hope to carry
that yellow blue talisman.
But this day I just pay attention

to the sparrows,
to steadying myself
in the steep melting snow,

to clearing brush until I finish,
to climbing back up the hill,
still in bright sun.

# Above Miami

My college daughter lives twenty-six stories
above Miami: high-rise white walls, low pile gray carpet,
one chair, a single O'Keefe print, tastefully framed,
towels and washcloths that match, a balcony soaring
above homeless streets, night breezes
of neon, bougainvillea, garbage.
Such simplicity shames my cluttered history:
shiftless closets, stuffed bottom drawers.

I dream I dump boxes of Christmas ornaments,
clothes I will never wear, off the balcony,
make my daughter's first grade spelling test
into a paper airplane and let it fly,
then grab the balcony railing, push off, free
of gravity, toward the sunrise Atlantic, green jungle,
blue ocean, Cuba, Hispaniola, Puerto Rico,
and finally, Senegal.

# II

# CHICAGO

# Leper

Concrete roaring in our ears after work,
we are so tired on the subway,
the papers screaming plunging markets,
drive-by shootings, one more thing
that causes cancer, we don't look up
when the man with running sores
and matted hair, smelling of old piss
and new whiskey, begins his plaint:
*Spare quarter? I need something to eat.*

No one looks him in the eye.
Some exhausted coins change hands.

# Sleeping on the El

She's maybe nineteen, old enough
to be my youngest daughter if I'd had another,
dressed hip in platform boots, quilted jacket for January,
seven silver rings on one hand, and one through her brow,
but her face is a baby's, sweet teenage
acne, little bow mouth.

She left State and Washington sitting straight,
headed for Loyola Station, with thoughts, a book, purpose,
but then the motion, the heat, the big scarf
she didn't really need, and now she's slumped,
innocent purse dangling from sleepy hands.

She surfaces, eyes open but glazed,
only at the stops, the sudden cold from
opening doors at Sheridan, Bryn Mawr, Granville.
Oh to sleep like that again, a gull resting

on waves, rocked by the universe,

to scrunch your body into easy comfort,

to feel your feathers, your hair, lifted gently

by the piss smelling wind,

# Antidepressants

Slowly the veil descends
between the world and my brain,
then becomes a picket fence.
Behind the fence the pill builds me
a temporary mud stick hut, dirt floor,
one round window, strangely flat
walls on which I hang pictures of
the Acropolis, the forest
of my childhood and Flamingo Beach.
The world does not go away,
just can't hurt me, for now.
I rest in the hut, eat strawberries,
watch the maple outside burn autumn red.
I pull up my Hello Kitty blanket,
sleep soundly, descend to the dream
cellar of good sex with strangers.
Even the wolves behind the fence are smiling.

## At Hancock Fabrics

Sewing is not a lost art among the African, Indian
women who prowl these aisles.

Outside:  concrete sky, cement snow falling and icy tongues
licking the windows opaque, obscuring potholed streets.

Inside:  forced air heat, dry fragrance of fabric,
one woman pressing peacock thread against her chosen cloth,

to see if it matches, even though she is already beautiful
in her turban, cape and scarf, beautiful like her baby

swathed in motley, dozing in the stroller,
eyes sometimes awake.

But like us all she wants more, something new, imagining
how her clever fingers will sculpt this cloth

into a shaped thing, a new thing for her baby,
and then, who knows, anything could happen.

At checkout she drops the thread.

I pick it up and hand it back.

Because we share no words she speaks a smile,
then wheels the stroller out with her purchased dreams.

I follow with mine, as she tucks in the baby,
covers her face with a scarf,

walks into the gray streets
of this foreign land, my home.

# Karaoke at the Glenway Tap

After Bill with his grandiose stomach
and Marlboros rolled into his sleeve
gets done slow dancing with Lisa,
the college girl with drop dead hips,

and after two telemarketers,
one secretary and a plumber make
a quartet to sing the songs they hear
in their heads, cars, the shower,

then Charlie in the shamrock polo shirt
sings *Danny Boy* faster than the digital music
and goes it alone at the end, without
video, words or back-up:

a cappella, *in sunshine or in shadow,*
*O Danny boy I love you so*,
sings to a bar hushed for ten brave seconds,
drinkers transported to the oldest, most incendiary,

longings, drinkers suddenly lost in green hills.

# Caroling at Clark St. Rehabilitation Center

At first we six feel awkward,
singing a cappella, missing harmonies,
forgetting easy ones like
*O Little Town of Bethlehem.*

And what business have we anyway
singing *Gloria in excelsis deo*
in front of darkening windows
in the lonely dayroom?

What business singing *Angels we have heard on high*
      to the six foot woman in an orange
      dress suit and matching hat?
      Or to the man with useless legs and a rose
      tattoo half visible under his rolled plaid sleeves?
      Or to the clear eyed one at the table
      whose face says *I do not want to be here?*

Then the aide says *sing along*
and some do—we relax into harmony.

The tattooed man sings all four verses
of *Joy to the World*, the last one solo:
*wonders of his love*
soaring in clear tenor.

# Scrubbing

Chicago in July has its own despair.
A southeast wind brings Caribbean
air, and humid clouds screw
a lid on the city, tight.

Just standing at a bus stop
breathing makes sweat spring from your armpits.
Exhausted dogs have gang meetings
on street corners, tongues dripping.

Even with scrubbing, your bathroom stinks.
In your kitchen, bananas are either green or rotten,
and the potatoes you bought last week, in hopes
of a salad, collapse into putrefaction.

You cannot remember why, from the depths
of February, you longed for summer.
You cannot remember why you ever
longed for anything.

# November

City squirrels are most beautiful now,
hopping across grass littered with wet leaves,
sodden Doritos bags, three of them
chasing each other around a tree trunk,
one running daintily on a wire,
all with luxurious tails, bodies fat and sleek
on the forgotten hotdog buns of summer,
the tomatoes pilfered from backyard gardens,
the occasional bag of peanuts;
one so bold he stands up straight
in front of you, paws folded
into his white chest,
demanding your sugar cookie.

But they are working too:
gathering, burying whatever is left,
scoping out tree holes, unkempt attics,
busy with scraps of insulation,
cardboard bits, lost string, all for nests,
busy working, knowing, like us,
what is to come.

# Advent: The Cook County Treasurer's Office

They put two hundred fake trees on the counter,
each three feet high, just enough to hide the employees,
each tree standing for a different place:
Ukraine weighty with jeweled satin balls,
Russia wearing sad-eyed little icons,
Japan light with origami and balsa wood,
the U.S. flaunting flags and stars,
and thousands of tiny lights
wound through them all.

At 4:30 even the guards are gone,
so I can rest my slush-stained briefcase
on the marble bench, after saying goodbye to Bob,
way back behind the trees, retiring after forty years.
The trees are all there is to look at.
An old woman with broken shoes
and a Macy's shopping bag is looking too, slowly,
one at a time. She says to me
*They're beautiful, aren't they?*

Yes, they are.

# Bread

Little cheer on the frozen beach
where January erases the line
between ice and white sky,
barren white except one patch
of darkwater heaving
a flotilla of gray gulls.

At home I packed my pockets
with all the generosity I have left.
Now I stop coughing for one second,
spittle freezing on ice, erasing
the line between bronchitis and pneumonia.
My father said pneumonia is friend of the old.

If not now, it will be soon.
I throw the bread. Seeing it spray,
some gulls gather, one hovers,
black white feathers fantailing
big wings in hummingbird beat,
reptile eyes demanding *give again*

and I do. He catches it on the fly,

hunger precise, beak cunning.

If soon, why not now?

So I sprout feathers, shrink my eyes,

fuse my teeth to a beak, grow small webs

between my toes, and fly to the darkwater,

out to the flock.

## January Afternoon

An appointment is suddenly cancelled,
an unscheduled time begins:
not breakfast with your friend
or a movie that starts at seven,
not swimming at the Y in the allowed period,
but time like finding a twenty in your jacket pocket
or that old sweater you really loved on the closet floor,
a gift of time to notice the sun's setting
a little later than December,
to see a beautiful boy with standup purple hair
and eight rings in one ear,
a time to remember the winter cardinal who endures it all
sometimes does pick the tree outside your window,
for no particular reason, to sing.

# On the Sill

Suddenly a mourning dove lands
on my fourth floor windowsill.
She cries low as she walks the concrete
against cold spring rain.

Always there is much to mourn:
piled bodies of Iraqis, Jews, babies
in the basement of Irish orphanages,
my parents dying alone in strange beds.

Still the dove chooses my window
a fitting place to roost, her reptile feet
tucking under her fluffed breast
as she settles, makes

my sill her brief home.
My breath evens. Things,
schedules, all bright follies,
fall away.

# Missing Snow

Everyone but me is so happy
for clear streets, dry yellow grass,
empty trees.

The weather people smile
in front of the cloud blanket map,
the dangerous lines and arrows

pointing south,
missing us again,
as they have all winter.

But I long for flakes
starting at four in February,
twilight glittering streets.

I miss the layered silence,
gathering by inches
in the darkest hours.

I want the blue white mornings,
every tree branch outlined,
every car mounded,

every bush bent, challenged,
nothing untouched under
the suddenly open sky.

# How to Survive Winter

The best way is to become a house cat:
focus on shrinking, growing fur.
work on the glow at the back of your retina,
teach your tongue to become bristly
and love fish scraps.

Second best, be like one:
keep yourself warm and clean,
practice curling up, sleeping
whenever you feel like it,
preferably on or near radiators.
Make your world small and soft,
thick with hairy pillows that smell like you.
Do only what must be done and savor it.
Smell the chicken soup as you open the can.
Lick the pan when done and
leave the washing until morning.
Learn to spend long hours staring
out of icy windows, waiting
for anything that moves.
Above all, remember no problem
cannot wait until Spring.

# Ducks

Three redheaded males with their soft brown mates
winter by the piled pier jutting
into Lake Michigan at the end of Pratt Avenue,
with the small rusty lighthouse
graffitied *fuck the world*.

Why not Florida or a corporate pond, someplace safe
from yelling seagulls flashing gang signs?
Why endure this beach so cold
they constantly sit in line,
fluffed up, beaks to the wind?

Why this lake with its double crosses,
sometimes freezing shore out, others horizon in,
sometimes tinkling shards, others sudden glaze?
Why don't their feet freeze
stuck overnight?

They always find open water,
even a ten foot circle half a mile out,
somewhere to paddle, dive down, miraculously re-emerge.

What can be feeding them from that darkness

to keep them fat, feathers sleek

and sufficient in the rising sun

as it moves north towards spring?

# Winter Rain

After the furious late winter rain
the morning dawns scrubbed clean.
The strengthening sun polishes the grass white.
The surviving squirrels tidy up
the trees so every ripple in the bark glistens.
They cluck in the branches, flap
their dust mop tails, warn of cats.
Above, the invisible sparrow choir
sings morning songs and the ice-free sidewalk
seems to lead somewhere
worth walking to.

# City by Water

After a cleansing rain and slow September sunset:
then stars, lighted towers to the west,
the black Lake upholding
this small yacht,

and for now the hustling streets,
sodden garbage, nervous briefcases,
outstretched begging hands, all disappear
into glittering skyline, dark waves.

The Great Lakes contain a fifth
of all fresh water on Earth.
Were all humans to vanish this night
all traces of the towers

except their ceramics, their plastics,
would be gone in fifteen thousand years.
But still tonight, where once was only
an onion field, now this architecture,

these fluorescent trains clattering

between buildings, this peninsular planetarium,

these hundreds of small harbored boats,

masts tinkling, waiting for dawn.

# Monet in Chicago

The four water lily paintings in a row
for the first time in a hundred years
speak not only of green noon swelling
to yellow three o'clock,

not only of turquoise six fading to gray eight,
but also of the patient eyes watching,
of the body brain at rest, awake under the tree
all afternoon, the only goal: to see.

So may I just sit
a quiet day by this great lake
in the city of my birth, see how
the limbs of swimming children

glisten in the shouting afternoon,
how heat breaks and shimmers across pavement,
how littered Coke cans shine treasure in the sand,
how between noon and eight there are at least

twenty-four shades of blue.

# Watching the Cubs in 2003

Even though they haven't won a pennant
since the year of my birth,
and they will lose again this year,
I'm watching again:

>because I love to scream in bars with other people;

>because in this Wrigley green field, pastoral on weekdays,
>a diamond island at night, bad things really do happen
>when you break the rules;

>because baseball's statuary breaks suddenly
>into ballet, the spotlight on the shortstop
>before he even knows;

>because they're gleaming muscled guys
>with names like Sosa, Martinez and Prior;

>because they get to spit on TV;

>because I can forget about the deficit, Medicare
>and Iraq for three hours;

because even though they can't hit,
their pitchers unwind fastballs leaving the batter dazed;

because once I, a girl and a lefty,
wasn't half bad;

because my left arm jumps a little,
aches with hope at the crack of Sosa's bat,

connecting, slamming a hurtling white ball
into clamoring Waveland Avenue.

# Sparrows

No one knows how they survive
the urban winter, how they really eat or live.
They chatter in the backyard evergreens,
or flock inside a chain link fence,
each a small brown monk
in his cell, head bent against the wind.

Without the jeweled colors of the endangered,
the migration sagas of geese or monarchs,
they are as common as dirt or the pleas
of the homeless for change, but tonight
while the first real snow falls, dry and driven
as sand across the alley streetlight,
tonight while I lay awake
with my usual demons,
sleep comes when I remember
in the morning I will spread bread.

# Napping by the Radiator

In my old cat Max I foresee our end:
what was once the backdrop to big things
becomes the big things.
He eats two bites of canned tuna, his former favorite,
then lumbers to the litter box, laboring an hour.
He spends the day in bed by the radiator
on the clean towel I put there,
safe, resting,
even though
       the sun splashes on the wall,
       the windowsill squirrels' chatter,
       the rolling tinfoil ball
all go unheeded, unchased.

When you apply for long term care insurance
the woman will ask you on the phone.
*Can you perform the eight activities of daily living?*
And you will say, wanting impossible future safety,
*Yes, of course,* fluffing your fur,
curling into the heat.

# The Old Woman Rides the Subway

She sees two women
who have swallowed basketballs,
remembers her one pregnancy long before
the bloody comings and goings gratefully stopped,
remembers his movement in her womb,
butterfly wings brushing walls.
So eager to come out, he punched
his way to the hospital.
It was only nine months.
He is fifty now.

The subway rocks her
into a nap where she dreams
her own bed and pregnant again.
But this time she must work it:
constantly talk him into
coming out, or he will retreat,
her belly flat again.
She wakes in tears, sweat, knowing
she has failed again, gets off
at Thorndale, the wrong stop,
begins the long limp home.

# December

Awake at three again, post menopausal gift,
I turn to radio jazz, ironic saxophones, exhausted love,
the deejay another sleepless human,
a friend in the night, like the one lit window
across my street, silent compatriot.

The sun has not shone here for sixteen days,
which are now only nine hours long.
The radio says snow, six inches south of I-80,
three inches up here, but only
cold rain slashes my window.

My mother died alone a year ago this night.

I pray for all the soldiers of the nation of this night;
for all those struggling to leave the world;
all those struggling to enter
(infant lungs squeezed into bursting light);
for the eternal safety of my children;

and finally for the blessing of snow:
each tree, every twig, outlined, heralded;
for that silent white gathering,
catching, holding, magnifying
what light there is.

# Darkness

This advent, after many deaths,
when the 5 p.m beast presses
its black flanks against the windows,
there will be no lighting of candles.
This advent, when the furniture fades to gray,
and the family photos disappear,
there will be no switching on of lights.
This advent, there will be no clanging carols,
no scurrying for basement boxes.
Instead only stillness,
letting whatever comes enter,
feeling darkness' peaceful fur brush by,
its soft breath hissing as the radiators clank to life,
its leaving of gifts, all with a hint
of frankincense, sometimes myrrh.

## Anniversary 40

Mine is basal cell, yours squamous,
neither one fatal, or even serious,
but still the cancer chasm yawns.
Cut, pulled and stitched,
we totter at its edge.
Now always the sun block, sometimes
the white lotion named *Efudex*:
home chemotherapy that first turns
the lesions red and sore,
then dry and harmless
as they fall away.

Though always tired in our bedroom
lit only by soundless late night TV,
we do this for each other:
apply it gently on our foreheads,
shoulders, the backs of our hands,
our fingers searching, finding
the raised edges, small bumps,
rubbing carefully into sleep
with a steady, circular motion.

# On the Red Line

Every workday I walk
the quarter mile to the elevated train,
to ride the beast that flashes, clatters
through my shattered sleep.

Some buildings live so close
to its tracks I could touch them:
January windows covered with taped newspaper,
shredded plastic foam dangling

from rusted air conditioners
no one had time to put away.
We are third floor, walk-up people,
who must hike many stairs to get home.

Maybe the night shift has it best:
in daytime the trains come only every fifteen minutes,
maybe allowing someone behind the paper walls
to settle into sleep, climb dreams.

III

CROSSING

# Baskets

I shot them in sixth grade, with mittens,
in sooty March twilight alone with a leaking ball
I'd nagged from my father:
shivering, bouncing, shooting from every spot,
retrieving it from the filthy ice, the mud.
Hour after hour, every day I could,
learning to run while bouncing,
then shoot off the backboard,
learning to leap, wait a nanosecond, then push,
*dribbling, lay up, jump shot,*
how the ball fit my body,
learning so well I knew when it left my hands
whether it would score, whether I would have
again that delicious delay when the net
holds the ball before it drops.

I made our little intramural team,
loved the cheering, passing, plays,
the sweat and the showers.
But the best that came of it
was the good knowledge,
fifty years later as I sink a free throw,

that for a long time the body is hard wired,

has no choices, must remember

what is has learned.

Then, of course, finally,

it does not.

# Jackie Deering is Dead

She had two asterisks by her name in the sixty dollar book
you can buy listing all the people who ever went to your high school.
Two asterisks. Meaning she's dead.
Her back-combed, bleached-white
hard sprayed hair, her skin tight skirts,
her Marlboros, blue nails, bathroom fights,
all dead.

She never listened to anyone and didn't
give a shit about her permanent record.
The last day I saw her was June 12, 1963,
sitting on a fast red Chevy, her graduation robe
already off, her killer legs dangling in the heat.
Our lives joined for one smile
through the haze of perfume, cigarette smoke, parents.
We knew it was the beginning.
We knew it was the end.

# By the Fire

I'm glad I had babies early
before I knew how
a bloody cord can strangle
how dark angel syndrome
can steal breath away

because I never
would have done it
would have missed

these people in my seventh decade
these people the smell
of their hair still brings tears
I can't be in the same room
without standing next to them
warming my thinning bones
by the clean fire of their bodies
singing always whatever mistakes
at least I did this

# Pine Lake

Though last year I swam across this half mile lake
whose only danger is its tangled weeds,
this year, at sixty, with drastically thinning bones,

I am afraid. I know too many ways to die.
Over my head. Panicked flailing,
water choked breath. Darkness.

Then I remember this is how the world begins
to shrink, stiffen. I've been swimming
fifty years, so I stuff fear

in my bathing cap and begin slowly, the easy strokes:
breast and side, rolling to back, the bowl of the sky,
the only sound my breath, heartbeat, arms,

the easy strokes, known from childhood.
I could do them in my sleep, and have,
and here the green hand of the lake

reaches up to hold me safe.

# The Woods of Home

In childhood I played
in a small wood, near home,
freely, as children did then, running
all paths in all seasons.

I didn't know the trees
by name, but I knew
January skeletons, April's softgreen net,
the canopy of August,

October's golden flags.
They taught me to be
alone with myself,
And even now, when my bones

are December twigs,
when I must step carefully over
all the roots of white oak,
black oak, cut maple, sugar maple,

when I enter the woods

my heart slows, my breath deepens,

the trees my best, lost, only

home.

## A Brief Season

In the few weeks of Midwest warmth,
before the leaf canopy closes
the sky until October,
the flowers of the forest floor take advantage:

may apples colonize a sunny hillside;
white trillium smother a small flatland;
bluebells lay claim to land along the path;
red and yellow columbine conclude
long negotiations with rocks,
emerge victorious from cracks.

There is too much of everything, too
many stamens to kiss all
the pistils. Fruits form quickly, seeds scatter
on wind, raindrops, the backs of squirrels.

Then it is over.
The seeds are crushed, smothered
in dead leaves, buried too deep.

Yet when Earth revolves again
out of darkness, some warriors
always sprout, white and tender.

# Right of Way

No one cares about the narrow
land next to the railroad,
summer thick with dandelion puffs,
crabgrass, thistles sprouting Kit-Kat packages,
blossoming aluminum beer cans.

Only the children come near,
clamber over broken pavement,
pipe pieces, glass shards,
to lay their ears on the warm track,
inhale the hum of the coming

hundred black car train,
bearing oil to the Gulf.
They lay their pennies and nickels
on the track, retreat. The train
screams by. They come out,

search and find the flattened copper
colored discs, the pewter ovals.
They don't see the derailment
ten miles down-track, but they

see the fire pillar, hear the sirens.

They do know pennies and nickels
don't derail, it's something else.
They don't know what to do,
so they walk home for supper, small miracles
of transformation jingling in their pockets.

# Chaco Canyon

The drifting hawk, descendant of dinosaurs,
dives for my mammal cousin, the mouse.
Her neck is broken and bloody before she is carried
away in talons. I saw her nest of babies yesterday,

blind mouths searching for tiny teats,
in their warm circle of shredded sagebrush.
They will be dead by sundown.
There is nothing I can do,

yet still tonight the ancient sky wheels
around Polaris, still the Dipper, Orion
and the burning myriad whose names I will never know
spin toward inevitable dawn.

# Siberian Sunbathers

In the *National Geographic* picture
the fat bikini women
stand smiling on the small
beach of the Ob River,

>which is not in the picture and
>which they can't swim in anyway,
>because, the caption says, it's the most
>polluted river in Asia.

Besieged by potato soup,
coal refineries, snow,
they blink into startling sunlight,
display their proud pale flesh
to the opening air
while the background buzzes
with sudden greenery, tundra flies.
Anorexia is not prevalent here.
Their hair is crinkly,
strong, not too clean.

They smile, smile

to the camera,

knowing these long days,

like all respites,

are brief

# Florida Keys

Suddenly insects as big as my thumb
roost in the screen door.
The Gulf and Atlantic squeeze the land
so narrow only one road runs
for two hundred miles, where things
grow and grow and never die,
the strident hibiscus big as a tree,
the crab whispering
*I am five hundred years old,*
which I don't believe for a second.
But still at night I can't stop dreaming
of the water beyond the shallow sea grass,
the water where the hammerhead shark
who lived at the mouth of the Tiber
when Rome fell, now long of tooth,
layered in cartilage, never sleeps.

# Antebellum

The house finished in 1861 burned
in a cigarette fire in 1890.
Twenty-three of twenty-nine columns remain:
a Roman forum ghosting in Mississippi woods.

Slaves built twenty-nine columns,
molded red bricks for the center
of each column, stirred heavy plaster,
shaped it around the bricks.

In 1863 its velvet parlors, book lined library,
became a makeshift hospital
where Union soldiers festered and died, just a stop
on the long march from Port Gibson to Vicksburg victory.

The placard lectures that members of the Daniell family,
who built it, are buried nearby, the earliest, one Frisby Frieland,
a Revolutionary War soldier, that *all men*
*are created equal: life, liberty*, etc.

A white boy and a black girl,
tattooed tourists, holding hands,

circle the house in gathering twilight,
reading the placards intently.

The graves of the slaves are everywhere, nowhere:
in wind-rustled treetops, in a cemetery in Chicago,
but mostly in the bricks, tortured muscles still flexing beneath,
breaking open the eroding plater skin of the columns.

# The Civil War Memorial in Byron, Illinois

Lincoln hailed from and Grant joined up from Illinois. Now its landscape festoons with concrete memorials to them, but not a single battle fought here, no Gettysburg, Atlanta, Vicksburg. The Illinois men marched off to other states. So says the cement obelisk, flanked by cannons, erected in memory of The Patriotic Boys of Byron, Illinois Who Fell to Subdue the Enemy. The faded names, readable only by touch, remember one John Hastings, Company F, 34th Illinois Infantry. Nothing to tell you John was seventeen, a private, brown hair, a farmer. Nothing to tell you Company F, 34th Illinois, crossed a rain softened field on 24 June 1863, near Shelbyville Pike, and halfway to their knees in mud drew the enemy from his position, with great courage and many casualties, including John. Death was dailier then, but did John's mother wake from a sound sleep at the moment of his death? Was his body brought back to Byron? Did his sweetheart and his sister frame a lock of his brown hair, for memory? In a hundred years the bumps of names will be flattened. The plaque on the obelisk says the two old cannons were restored in 1997, but no skirmish, not even a holding action, to save the eroding names.

# Just Summer

Stewart Lake is really a pond, of course,
no manatees, dolphins, big turtles,
not even sturgeon, trout or perch,
nothing endangered, worth studying, or even big.

Just flocks of minnows near shore
and a common gray brown fish,
narrow, the length of your hand,
lightly bumping your thigh

as you push into the blessed warm water
of this little lake surrounded
by squat cottages with
cracked linoleum kitchens,
crumbling roofs, overstuffed couches smelling
of years of wet bathing suits.

You push past the sandy shallows
where little girls in a hurry
have peed for many summers,

then push into deeper water,
begin your old Australian crawl:
the ferris wheel shafts of sunlight,
the silver coins of light
break from your arms and hands.

# An Old Woman at Cancun

She sits alone and still in simple pearls,
basic black dress, slightly rouged cheeks,
observing the young: flirting,
drinking margaritas in the hotel bar.
No one sees her, except the Mexican
bartender, who bestows the smallest of smiles.
Her husband is in the room, finishing
his trembling shave. She came out here
because she couldn't stand it anymore,
It is hard, harder every year.
But now she too tries a small smile.

# The House of Old Age

has only four rooms:

>to eat,
>
>to bathe,
>
>to sit,
>
>to sleep;

>doors that click shut,
>
>ten books,
>
>one pan,
>
>four bowls,
>
>three pillows,

and windows everywhere:
no curtains or shades,
windows sliding open
easily to catch
the chariot sun.

## Small Things

No one told me how to be old
and happy, or if they did, I did not listen.
No one told me my old life would die.
Standing on the bridge, smothered
in my sour winter coat, I follow flooded twigs
and leaves floating on high water beneath.
My lungs squeeze sorrow at children
running the woods, cartwheeling
sodden lawns, biking rainy hills.

I still have stringent morning coffee,
goldfinches splashing the birdbath,
blond tailed squirrels swinging from the feeder,
sometimes a contrail sunset, and
the stretched solitude of a lap swim:
all small buds maybe blossoming
into a new life, a *nova vita*
of sorts.

## Dia de Los Muertos

The media holiday is immigrant profound,
like the wan, lacy Madonna born through
1900 Italian streets, only this time
altars to Elvis: seven plastic guitars

and velvet embroidered sideburns.
Or a shrine to a brother stabbed by gangs:
diploma, jeans, running shoes,
bags of Oreos, cans of Mountain Dew.

This holiday's right about the important thing:
the dead do not inhabit graveyards, churches, séances.
They want their stuff.
They miss their only home.

So, to celebrate Dia de Los Muertos,
find that ring he wore for thirty years,
drink tea from that hand painted china cup
she loved, the one with

the black and yellow bird,
rescue his rusty trowel to bury your bulbs,

feel its heft in your hand.
and the dead will rise full-bodied

like Proust's childhood from his madeleines.
They will rise on Dia de Los Muertos.
They will eat your heart.
They have no choice.

# March Sunset

Cold hardens the world.
All ice piles gray and filthy.
All trees tangle empty brown.
Then for fifteen minutes comes
oblique light burnishing
faded grass, beautifying
the slovenly plastic Christmas wreath
left over on the window next door,
gilding the feral fur of the cat
who licks her merciful plate clean.
For fifteen minutes the inside
of your house shines.
The old pictures of your
relatives smile again.
This sunset does not
promise spring.
It promises nothing,
asks only
that you see.

# Common

I.     *Daylilies*

They sneak up in June, grassy leaves appearing overnight,
stalks a few days later, laddered with fat buds
bursting orange into daylight,
twisting closed at sunset, always spreading,
colonizing lawns, invading woods, rocky hills,
whatever they can get.
They need no weeding, watering, mulching,
will conquer crabgrass, Creeping Charlie,
everything they meet, heedlessly,
democratically, decorating the land.

II.     *Squirrels*

The ones hopping across July lawns
might or might not be the ones from last fall,
the ones who dutifully buried
secret food at the base of trees.
Their nests of babies, writhing piles
grasping for milk, are mostly hidden,
their dead seldom seen, other than road kill.

Never mind, summer blooms short and now
they chatter and scold from branches and wires,
flaunting their feather boa tails,
ears upright, eyes ablaze.

III.     *Sparrows*

They winter over without the cardinals' red coats,
the chickadees' black caps, dressed only
in their brown grey coats from the Salvation Army.
They live mostly on handouts: thrown bread
or the few seeds left in feeders
the big birds didn't get.
At night they huddle in hedges,
fluff up against the wind.
On February mornings warm enough
to melt the birdbath water,
they flutter down for a drink and a shower,
still alive in faint sunlight,
snapping their feathers.

# Thursday Night

The bear of desire once stood
full height, crashed through trees
to smear her muzzle with salmon,
blackberries, whatever she wanted.
Now she is a cub and scares easily.
We send her an invitation
on linen stationery: the pleasure
of your company is requested
Thursday, April 2, 9:30 p.m.

We are glad for freezing rain
that night. She will want shelter.
She will join us, soft paws
up the stairs, nosing the bedroom door
open as we blanket burrow deep.
Wind shakes the house.
Rain slashes windows.
Touch me, old love, only love,
touch me so we know
each other again.

# Annunciation in Northern Illinois

September: all garden work done,
now just sitting in angled afternoons
among humble annuals:
marigolds, impatiens, zinnias.
But then the hummingbird,
he of purplegreen back,
sips zinnias in sunset fire.
Here he is mostly rumor,
but today a herald stopping
face level, angelic whirring
a suspended salutation, breathless.
And though I have not been a virgin
in body or mind for many years,
I know at last I have found favor.

# Corn

In Illinois it should be knee high
by the Fourth of July—
not to the shoulder,
industrially sown, pumped with nitrogen,
rows marching too close,
ranks filing up and down
the small hills, nothing like
the lazy open columns
we once pushed aside
for crunchy teenage sex.

Yes, the nitrogen infects the Mississippi,
finally floods the Gulf
with algae blooming dead zones;
yes, it's the base of fattening fructose,
stinking feedlots and all that meat.
But still the land, once tangled
prairie, gives whatever we ask for,
still, this enormous green.

## three screws

the sun comes up whether or not I've slept and at first light winter red cardinals empty the bird feeder throwing out for the helluvit a few sunflower seeds that sparrows or squirrels will eat and thus survive and my fear of death can't stop the March light from lengthening and has no effect whatsoever on the river ice melting and breaking and my knee having no meniscus and my hip held together with three screws the mushy snow doesn't give a rat's ass about when I clamber through it fall and get up again and even though my friend's son killed himself two days ago the little vixen fox living behind the garage will eat the slowest mouse crunch his bones to the marrow all of which is somehow infinite comfort to me and I know my head swelled with grief and anger is just an appendage of neurons synapses and earth from space a bluegreen ball spinning into indifferent darkness

# Broken

The bird is not sitting right,
too low in the frosted grass,
something broken: his green black wing
or iridescent neck or hidden feet,
his eyes blank staring at the hedge
he will never reach.

When a hunted deer's sharp hoof
kicks a California mountain lion
just right to break his jaw,
he slinks to rock crevasses,
his eyes empty
as this bird's, waiting.

The sun rises, spewing light
on the cheap daffodils by the hedge,
on the entire fallen world,
the only one we have,
on the breast of this dying bird.

# Luke 24: 36-42

He could not give up the flesh.
In the moments before we leave forever
we want to say what he did:
*I have hands, feet, bones; touch me,*
*and is there anything for breakfast?*

We are tethered to tubes,
nails hammered hard,
spear in our side, soon
to pass through, but still
*this is my body,*

with the scar on my hand from the bike accident,
the lungs shredded with chemo,
the broken left foot never quite healed,
but still all I have ever known:
*this is my body.*

If I rise, let it be not
as a ghost, no metaphor
for new life; please something
like this body, some flesh,
something I can understand.

# Deer in Town

Shotguns blast the gray air, shatter
the skeletal trees of the state park forest.
Some deer come to town knowing
it is safe, vanishing in our small,
scattered woods, seen only if they move.
Two does nuzzle down a hill, eating
whatever is still green, shining noses
and flippant tails sometimes
giving themselves away.
My stare locks on one doe's
huge eyes. She is not afraid,
a fellow creature gazing back
for one instant.

# Jonquils

The water always begins us,
soaks our bulb skin,
swelling us tight.

What can we do but push
through winter death:
grey grass, windblown sticks.

We must reach for light
to sprout our yellow trumpets,
golden collars, to release
our first fragrance
in the few days of our life.

They call us Narcissus,
but were there a pool next to us
we would not bend
to see our reflection.
We do not come for ourselves, for you.
We have no choice,
which is why you love us.

# Voyager Enters Deep Space

We launched her almost forty years ago
with pictures of us: naked, hands raised
in the universal greeting *hello*.

She carried a golden disk etched with
Beethoven's 5th, *No Satisfaction*, tones of didgeridoos,
with voices saying *hi* in Swahili, Chinese, French.

She carried with her a map marking
*where we come from*, all nine planets,
an arrow shot from the third one out.

We launched her to slingshot
around Mars, Neptune, Uranus. For billions of miles
she sent back pictures of exploding light.

We know now she's left our small system,
bombarded by strange particles, a human artifice
drifting through dark infinity, bearing the real message:

*We are lonely.*

Made in the USA
Columbia, SC
15 April 2018